Some Dogs Drown

A Collection of Written Works by

Joseph R. DeNatale

Napa County Youth Poet Laureate

Ideas into Books®: Westview
Kingston Springs, Tennessee

Ideas into Books®
W E S T V I E W
P.O. Box 605
Kingston Springs, TN 37082
www.publishedbywestview.com

ISBN 978-1-62880-265-8 Perfect bound
ISBN 978-1-62880-266-5 Case laminate

First edition, May 2023

Photo credits: Front cover photo, back cover collage, and collage
photos by Joseph DeNatale; Back cover photo of the author by Tanner
Carmichael; Author photo on page 59 by Tyler Diehl.

Digitally printed on acid free paper.

Foreword

My name is Marianne Lyon. I have been the poet laureate of Napa County, California for the past three years. My background is that I have been writing poetry for many years and I have 240 poems published in various literary magazines, journals, and reviews including Ravens Perch, Leaping Clear, Slippery Elm, and Black Fork Review. I am also honored to be a member of the California Writers Club, Solstice Writers in St. Helena, CA, and Cofounder of Wordsmiths of Yountville, CA.

It is with this background that I tell you about the high regard I have for the poetry of Joseph Raymond De Natale, who was named the first-ever teen poet laureate of Napa County in 2021.

I found Joseph's poems very moving. He exhibits literary skill in utilizing a unique awareness of words as more than just a way to convey meaning. I am struck by the way the lines flow; the writing shows the use of subtle rhythm which lends a "singing" quality to the work and that is what shapes the poem.

For many teenagers, the pandemic (as well as world events and the political climate in our country) caused loss, fear, depression, and anxiety. Joseph did not escape these consequences. In my review of some of his poems, there is a sense of loss that is captured not just by the word choices but the awareness and use of the "weight" of his words. I believe that Joseph's poems will resonate with many teens or young adults who have also suffered the residual effects of the pandemic and other stressors. Moreover, I believe that his poems will be impactful on a broader audience of readers of all ages.

I am uplifted by Joseph's collection of poems. He is clearly brave and bright. I believe he will draw you in, as he did me, so that you will be fully engaged with his poetry and leave with respect and understanding.

Marianne Lyon

Table of Contents

1 – Every day is a series of breaths

3 – Going away party

5 – In dreams

7 – Plane Crash over Clear Lake, Iowa

9 – Mourning in October

11 – 9PM pacific standard time

13 – Both Ways

15 – Ten Feet

17 – The Catalyst

19 – A mirror to Sunday

21 – Temperance

23 – Strange Ruminations of a Waking Mind

25 – San Pablo Inn Rotisserie Club

27 – Sunday, through the back door

29 – Requiem for a soul ablaze

31 – Steel

33 – No Blood pt. 1

35 – No Blood pt. 2

37 – The Beast

39 – Some Dogs Drown

41 – The Ballad of Saratoga Downs

43 – Early morning on Mt. Tom with Grandpa

45 – Miss California, was built for Ohio

47 – Valley of the Moon

49 – The Feeling

51 – The Labyrinth

53 – Synopsis

55 – Sleepwalking

Every day is a series of breaths

in and out,
to and from,
beginning and end
and middle
and over again

we drive to the outskirts of the city
then drive back
silently resigned to these roads,
i need them like air
retracing my steps back
and forth
like deep breaths
to calm my shaking hands

i wonder when i'll let go,
breathe it out,
release it into the atmosphere
and then, pause
hoping it will come back to me,
filling my lungs again

like air,
i took it for granted
and it polluted my soul.

Going away party

why are your bags out front?
it doesn't make any sense
i wonder if any small change
would have rearranged it all
but wondering is a stupid game to play;
it does no good dwelling on the past
throwing "ifs" around to see if they will stick
asking: why are your bags out front?
i only blinked and now you're gone
not for lack of love
but it never slows down
time marches on
i used to muse that life was
"one big going away party"
these days it only feels truer
and i'm left to wonder,
why are your bags out front?

In dreams

in dreams
only there you'll speak to me
in distant smiles
in fading memories

in dreams
that leave me up haunted for days
in photographs
that i can't bear to throw away

in dreams
where all is right in the worst way
in years gone by
in every single yesterday

in dreams
where i would often rather stay
in words we spoke
in the meaning of a phrase

in dreams
only there you'll speak to me
in distant smiles
in fading memories

Plane Crash over Clear Lake, Iowa

it's only fantasy
pretending to know what i want
because eventually
knowing and creating feelings become all the same
and there is no separation any more
detachment from myself
detachment from everything
i am an island
i am a desert island
i watch planes fly overhead
i know they see me
i watch the chemtrails paint my name
across the sky
but i know they do not know me
and that they'll never fly close enough to
i don't sleep often
i spend most nights
getting to know the worst parts of myself
but when i do sleep
in the early hours of the morning
i sometimes dream
i dream that one day
a plane comes down from the sky
but when i wake up
all i see is the smoke
of a distant plane crash

Mourning in October

the autumn breeze is fairer to me than the faces of
the crowds
i go walking by myself when everyone has settled
down
my company is bitter like the chilling of the wind
i find no solemn comfort upon reflecting deep
within

i am just the reaper of the fate that i have sown
a long and empty journey that i have to face alone
i argue with myself at times, looking for a cause
i give myself no answer to the reason for my loss

knocking at the door of my own consciousness
there i stand
a question on my mind
and no one left to grip my hand

a question on my mind
and no one left to grip my hand

9PM pacific standard time

it's the middle of the day in china
and it's 9PM here
it's the middle of the day in china
and that doesn't matter to me at all
i can't focus on anywhere else
i seem to focus on anything other than myself
i never thought the world revolved around me
i always seemed to revolve around the world
spinning in circles through the day
turning in circles through the night
moving from room to room
until it no longer makes sense
but even when it no longer makes sense
the cycle continues
blissfully unaware of its surroundings
leaving me behind but stuck in its wake
until i am close to back where i began
but it's 9PM here
it's the middle of the day in china
and i wonder who i will be by that time tomorrow

Both Ways

it only goes both ways
i'm only limited to freedom of choice
i'm only limited
it only goes both ways
and it isn't a loop
at least loops make sense
it's a one way street that goes two ways
and i am standing at either end
so my choice is already made
it only goes both ways
the past into the future
and the future into the past
it all melts together
until i stumble into tomorrow
losing sight of yesterday
and wondering why
it only goes both ways
like walking back and forth
in the dead of night
and getting lost
while knowing where i am because
it only goes both ways

Ten feet

winter is hard
treading water
trying not to drown
i seemed to float just fine back then
i seemed to float
but maybe it only looked that way from
ten feet below
that maybe sometimes the light plays tricks
and it could never be only sun rays

The Catalyst

i am the house
that they built in the country
and you are the freedom of being alone
i am the wood that the house it was built with
and you are the house when it's still not a home

i'm indecision
the doubt that you're left with
and you are the certainty that I may need
i am the safety net
you were the catalyst
i've never known what it's like to be free

i am the movie
that's on in the next room
and you are the walls
which are so very thin
i am the clock that's behind in the kitchen
and you are my mind that's an hour ahead

i'm apprehension
the fear of beginnings
and endings and everything else in between
i am the starlight
and you are what's made of them
i only ask that you say what you mean

i am December
you're everything after
and this is the part that we wish wasn't true
i am the ember
that jumped from the fire
you opened the door and you let me right through

you are the answer
the unspoken question
that rests in the very dark parts of my soul
i was the taxi cab
you were my passenger
i pulled the wheel and i lost all control

A mirror to Sunday

i remember what i'd do
on days like this
and sometimes
i can't even open my mouth to speak
my head feels so suffocating

i wonder who you are sometimes
i wonder who anyone is
through my eyes it all just melts together
and the real and the fake
don't differentiate much any more

when i think about you
my thoughts go blank
when i think about you i laugh
my laughter isn't real
it's only how i want to react
because it's all just one emotion
and it tips and falls apart
i am not who i was
when we stood at the start

i remember last night
i remember shaking hands
i remember a snide comment
that took me by surprise
don't we all love honestly
until it bites us back

and it's fun to live with disregard
until your words start to count
your words never counted
always opposed to mine

Temperance

there's a moment when you realize
the silence isn't temporary
everything is temporary
it just depends for how long

how it feels to fall apart
again and again
but stay structured by an involuntary force
dragging me along
sometimes awake
and at other times in a fog
that focuses my eyes
on the horizon
and my tongue to the bottom of my mouth
how it hurts to speak
and sometimes to stay silent

a tempered reminder in the corner of my room
that i am in control of the ending
but maybe it's better to leave control out of my
hands

Strange Ruminations of a Waking Mind

i had a thought,
sitting in the bitter early hours
of a darkened room
i had a thought and it buried itself
deep inside my conscience,
cemented itself in my head

driving over roads until I erode them down,
pounding against gravel
over and over and over
until it no longer fights back

sometimes it rains
and other times i watch the sky
for hours
with no sign of movement
fall is here again,
bittersweet and without escape

in the morning
winter reminds me
that it is just around the corner;
ready to strike at once,
biding time with its razor sharp teeth
bared

this type of weather used to mean heartbreak;
now it only means solemnity, acceptance
an emotion dug up and beaten
and buried once again

can you count the stop signs on the way back to your
house

i promise i'll act like i never saw them

The San Pablo Inn Rotisserie Club

by the time i wake up once more
my dreams will have melted
and soul separates from soul again
but the intertwining melodies
will not let me relax
turning on my back and losing sleep
and running till i'm out of energy

i can feel it again
crawling in through the cracks
that I have widened just to seal
a chance to feel real
or to disappear again

in between my eyes
a recollection of my finer memories
disappears
last week into last month
last month into eternity
staying stagnant is impossible
because the world will move through you
say goodbye to tomorrow,
leave time in the early hours for yesterday
and never understand now

how we danced back and forth
and only for a moment met in the light
only for a moment

Sunday, through the back door

often i catch myself staring
at something in the distance-
i'm unsure what it is.
but my eyes slip past
the marble countertop adorning my kitchen,
the last golden streams of light
basking lazily across its face;
signifying the end of the day.
and once more past the back door
and over the garden fence
and then:
the horizon.
maybe it's out there,
hidden somewhere in the iridescent skyline.
or maybe i'm looking past it,
through it,
at some unknown object lying just out of sight.
gradually my eyes slip back,
over the fence,
through the door,
across the counter,
and settle abruptly at my feet.
only a moment's respite
from the rest of my troubles,
a reocurring, aimless notion
content to fade to the back of my mind
and pay me a visit another day.

Requiem for a soul ablaze

a mountain just like that one
a heart just like yours
someone sits and watches from
the peak
knowing any and all words
eventually become useless

it's too dark to figure anything out now
we'll wait until dawn
someone's losing sleep
and mumbling through the night
reminiscing on yesterday
without acknowledging a single moment
that came before

a glimpse of the
bitter and bright morning sky
reflecting through dirty glass
sending a chill down
someone's spine
what came and devoured the trees
still burns here

a rusted metal gate
separating me from nothing
a line i won't cross
and a memory i won't look back on
until next November
when i've already forgotten
who i am

Steel

sadness isn't an emotion
it is a dark and expansive valley
that i have walked through many times;
a hollow I have resolved to shut the door on,
to ignore its careful lull for good

to be cold, hard, unfeeling steel

the cyclical routine brought on by daybreak
begins anew, yet it has no effect on me
i have detached myself at the root,
cut and hacked away at what i thought
tethered me to the earth,
and when I sliced through the last stalk

 i became cold, hard, unfeeling steel

outside the sky opens up and begins to weep
with the intensity of a grieving mother,
thrusting rain down from above in biblical fashion
ice cold bullets whipping against my face,
streaming down my cheeks like wasted tears,
the kind that will never come again

now i am cold, hard, unfeeling steel.

No Blood pt. 1

it's like these days i can barely keep
my eyes open
and really – what's the point?
it's like having the same conversations
telling the same jokes
singing the same songs
traveling around and around and around
and somehow
circling back to yesterday's steps
caught up in the darkened space between
two contrasting thoughts
pacing the back rooms of an empty
storefront
reminiscing is only ever fun in the end
serving more as a reminder of what was lost
than anything else
and isn't that the most fitting punishment?
everything lost to time;
reason, beauty, blame
she has taken the knife
and cut swiftly through the bone

no blood

No Blood pt. 2

the truth is sometimes you grow up
and nothing changes
and it is silent for a moment
sometimes an old friend
catches the corner of your mind
and lingers without cause
when resolution becomes a privilege,
a fantasy
like the reruns they show
when everyone's parents are finally
asleep
defaulting to near constant confusion
split down the middle by
intermittent epiphanies
that come twice as slow as they
disappear
and there is always someone out there
with the answer
but the joke is
you will never find them
where can you even turn your back this time of
year?
the knife twists and yet

no blood

The Beast

"that's just the way it is these days"
heard in passing
heard at the coffee shop
down the street and a mile right
from my house

there's something about acceptance,
finding solemn comfort
in the cold embrace of hopelessness
it's not right is it?
to lay down and die?
to scream one last prayer
and then, in an act of utter defiance to
wrestle the hands of fate off of the
steering wheel
and take the sharpest possible left,
feeling the wheels lift and spin and dance
and then, like all things,
eventually plummet directly towards
whatever they teach is at the bottom?

or is that the answer?
maybe we lost the moment
we decided that fighting back was worth it

and maybe not all of this was gleaned
from the simple words in the coffee shop,
but more from the man's intention;
from the way he will drive home
and he will go to sleep
and when he wakes up
he will not worry about the
moment before he dies
but instead a thousand different things,
menial tasks and meaningless interactions,
cold stares and sharp indecision,
love and pain and beauty
and everything he will never have
no matter how hard he tries

and in the end
this is what will eat him alive
that is the beast hiding in the closet
it is him
and the life he has made

Some Dogs Drown

it's like
there is ALWAYS someone
waiting for me in the basement
but they don't want to ruin the surprise.
i guess i shouldn't blink then,
even though every moment
eventually becomes one wasted,
lost to time.
retracing my steps,
i find that only my most potent regrets
will dare utter a word,
and it leaves me wondering
if it is possible to appreciate the present
when it has recklessly devoted itself to becoming the
past.
there's something about
the colder months of fall,
about abandoned houses,
about loss;
winter has stretched its hand out now.
yesterday, i sat outside all evening
and counted the things I was afraid of
until it was too dark to see them;
and a thought arrived in my mind:
"even in a perfect world,
some dogs drown."

The Ballad of Saratoga Downs

do you think
you would recognize the moon
if it approached you
in a room full of stars?

some mornings,
i struggle to know myself
the mist only begins to fade
around mid-afternoon
and by evening
i am disillusioned once again
by the malevolent spirit of the night

"turn around"
says some sign or figure of authority
and maybe that would have swayed me
back then
but every day it is increasingly clear
that the only option now is to push forward
to speed recklessly ahead
and shut my eyes
and brace for impact,
one that never arrives
because the road only continues,
narrow straits and blind turns

"in half a mile, your destination will be on the left"
but there never really was anywhere to go
and most days the best option is to turn
around,
to admit defeat and concede
to whatever force is pulling me back,
back towards the center of your heart

lord grant me the strength
to one day break free
to find my place among the vines
and fig trees
to expel what semblance of myself
was left over after the final bell rang,
to lay down
and shut my eyes
and brace for impact

Early morning on Mt. Tom with Grandpa

the half second before a thought appears,
before it is even fully formed,
a split moment of regret
and just like that it can't be undone

i should really be thankful
for the way we communicate;
if everyone spoke in truth
we would lose all ambiguity,
the bitter sense of mystique that gives
life any meaning

it's like the sharp snap of a twig
off a beaten dirt path
somewhere in the mountains
of central California
it's possible that you could
get stuck in the valley for years:
like falling asleep at 5AM
and waking up in a cold sweat half past three
i guess the feeling never goes away
it just cements itself into reality
as you grow older

i always thought the past would
smile back with a certain fondness,
not sink its resentful claws into
the pit below my heart and swallow me entirely

would it be fair to say that disappointment
is as integral to the human heart as joy?
is suffering inherent?
or do we simply make the waking choice
to endure it,
in the hopes that one day we will be
compensated for our efforts;
rewarded for the time we spent
attempting to spend our time
Correctly

Miss California, was built for Ohio

what beast do you seek to become?
in the winter everyone's doors are locked
and passing smiles
are replaced by cold stares
does connection waver?
does connection exist?

keep me guessing at your intentions,
at the moment they become tangible
they are no longer yours
everyone's a thief these days
so nothing is really ever stolen
only passed
from hand to mouth and back again
until the game loses itself
loses meaning, structure
anything of note

stripping the hood back
sometimes reveals nothing
sometimes when something is broken
all that means
is that it has stopped working
sometimes the brain dies before the heart,
sometimes the body dies before the soul
and isn't it that way with all things?

all coexistence is temporary,
as the mind shifts and warps with time
flowing and bending and nearly snapping
we were never meant to last
nothing more than a breath, a fleeting shadow
a shifting stone in a stream that flows out
somewhere far into the deep

Valley of the Moon

valley of the moon
like needles in my broken back
valley of the moon
the lines between the white and black
don't make it any clearer
well it's fading by the day
in the valley of the moon
everything will waste away

life just isn't fair
everyone knows and no one cares
try and catch it by the hair
the corner wall, a broken mirror
tell me that you know
what i never got to say
in the valley of the moon
no one real is ever safe

turn your back on time
it keeps moving forward right down the line
a whisper in my mind
that tears me right up and leaves me behind
just give me one more look
telling me you understand
in the valley of the moon
there are only empty hands

valley of the moon
like roads that seem to lead nowhere
valley of the moon
like a shadow that was always there
it's never getting clearer
it's only ever fading by the day
in the valley of the moon
everything will waste away

The Feeling

it's like a flash in the pan,
one last spark shooting high up into the sky
before the grand inevitable darkness;
the type that isolates you against the world,
dampening your vision
and leaving you longing for connection

it's all the people you will ever talk to
in one room
for some kind of celebration;
the type where you shift from
conversation to conversation
an endless barrage
of goodbyes and hellos
like entrances and exits
in a poorly written play;
the type you perform
with a children's choir
at the church downtown

it's climbing up on the old gym
half past midnight
and wondering if it really does change
beyond those mountains
or if it's just one big echo chamber,
a singular heartbeat resounding
against the steep valley walls of my skull;

the type of thought that stubbornly
refuses to leave, chained to a large oak tree
at the end of the main street of my mind

it's the question i came
with the intention to ask
before the words got caught in my throat
and my thoughts got caught on
a conversation overhead by the curb
the type that no one will mention the next day,
for good reason.

The Labyrinth

what is left of me,
stripping away the sum of my parts?

always chasing some abstract definition
of perfect,
i exhaust myself wholly
finding as i grow older that
ignorance truly is bliss,
that the acknowledgement
of any given problem really
only ever makes it worse

to live blind to pain and sorrow
is to live blind to joy and love,
but to live blind is to live freely;
condemned by my existence
to a life shackled up against
expectations and obligations,
deadlines and decisions

i wake to unquiet darkness,
sore from wrestling with my mind
never actually able to gain the upper hand

lacking permanence in thought,
it seems every day
is some grand new revelation,
in our endless quest for knowledge
we begin to think that just as
we know nothing, we know everything

and so we chew and spit back out
the same meaningless epiphanies
masquerading as genius

a note from the editor:
"you are losing control of your language.
could it be that you are working
too hard to revisit ideas
you've already worked through?"
i assume he's correct,
in the way that i assume there
is good in the heart of
every passing face i encounter,
and every hand i hold

Synopsis

the advantage
to killers who are patient
the synopsis won't
always write itself
understanding
just how far you can take it
that's what loss is
when no one's left to tell

i miss love
and feeling like it mattered
any day now
the feeling starts to change
from above
it hits you like a shower
hope it stays
all you can do is pray

i miss rage
when something's so important
i'm self righteous
i'm human at the most
it's okay
as long as you don't forget
there's nothing like it
as far as living goes

don't give praise
especially if you really mean it
these ovations
keep standing up to me
these days
i find i'm having trouble seeing
between faces
and knowledge and belief

Sleepwalking

i carefully study every action i take
so that it doesn't end up
as a mistake later on
it's like counting the steps down
to the mailbox and back
and expecting the number to change

at night i walk circles around myself
and wake up exhausted
the other evening i closed my eyes
and found myself walking the empty halls
of an elementary school i didn't go to,
and when
i opened my eyes and i was sitting
in the garage of an old friend,
my hands freezing

there's a mountain somewhere
calling my name
and i'd drive there if i could
but all my friends are too tired
so once again Sunday brings
sullen disappointment,
waking up to find the house empty

i find myself in the presence of others
and find that there's never any good time
to be in the presence of myself,
except for the darkest hours of morning
when dad gets in his electric car
and drives to work
i think about how he used to drive a truck
and how some things were always meant to change

permanence is some grand myth;
knowing that tomorrow the world ends,
that yesterday was the best days of your life
and that the bittersweet in between
is fading every day

About the Author

Joseph Raymond DeNatale was born and raised in Napa, California. He has been writing poetry for ten years and in 2021 was named as the first-ever Napa County Youth Poet Laureate. Joseph spends most of his time enjoying or creating music and film. He is the songwriter and lead singer of two bands: the Turtlenecks and Excluding Humans, both of which have songs on all streaming platforms. Joseph has participated in Congressman Mike Thompson's Student Leadership Council, where he and his peers led a climate change conference.

Joseph resides with his parents and two sisters in Napa.

Photo by Tyler Diehl

9 781628 802658